Praise for

Instant Relevance

D1531623

"We, as educators today, must compete with what is going on inside students' heads, and we are losing. It's not that students aren't highly engaged with the world around them. Today's students are savvier than ever and very engaged in the world in which they live. The problem is that this engagement is not taking place at school.

"Denis's book, *Instant Relevance: Using Today's Experiences in Tomorrow's Lessons*, can change all of that tomorrow. In this book, Denis has provided numerous examples of how to engage students of all ages, while actually at school. No longer must students wait until the bell rings to be excited about learning. My only hope is that my children's teachers purchase a copy of Denis's book. Better yet, I think I will purchase one for them.

"Denis's blend of practical application, expertise, and humor make this book like few I have ever read. He will teach you how to sneak learning into lessons using regular, everyday moments. The cool part is that your students will not even see it coming, but in the end, they will be asking for more."

—Jon Harper, assistant principal,
blogger for Bam Radio and host of *My Bad*

"Holy cow, this book is good! Every single teacher should read this. Denis is *funny*. This book is an easy read, relevant, and will transform your teaching."

—Alice Keeler, teacher, speaker, and author of
50 Things You Can Do with Google Classroom

"Our professional and personal lives are inherently connected. In *Instant Relevance: Using Today's Experiences to Teach Tomorrow's Lessons*, Denis Sheeran looks at the things that he sees every day and connects them to the lives of his students. He makes these day-to-day observations seem "instantly relevant" to his students and those around him with thoughtful insight and rich storytelling. This book encourages educators to look at our world differently and make every day relevant to our students, so when they ask, "How am I going to use this in real life?". . . We have an answer.

"After reading Denis Sheeran's *Instant Relevance: Using Today's Experiences to Teach Tomorrow's Lessons*, I have begun to think differently. I now look at the day-to-day as a teaching opportunity, instead of just passing it by."

—Jay Billy, elementary school principal

"In education, engagement is the key to relevance. More than 'am I going to use this in the future,' students want to know whether they're going to find something interesting and engaging right now. And Denis Sheeran's *Instant Relevance* is packed full of classroom-tested strategies for engaging students in powerful and meaningful ways.

—Michael Fenton, teacher, Lead Instructional Designer, Desmos

"Denis Sheeran provides readers with pedagogically sound insight on what math instruction should look like in the year 2016. The countless real world examples shared in the book provide readers with a plethora of learning experiences that can be implemented immediately. Readers' own professional growth will be elevated from reading *Instant Relevance* and ultimately impact the success of students."

—Brad Currie, Billy Krakower, and Scott Rocco,
Founding Partners of Evolving Educators LLC

"Practical. Essential. Humorous. What else do you need? *Instant Relevance* encapsulates the aspect of teaching necessary to make a classroom successful: relationships + real world = success. That means relationships among teachers and students, as well as making connections between learning and the real world. Sheeran's book is a must-read for educators who are looking to transform their classrooms, by turning everyday material into lessons that matter to students and stretch them as learners."

—Sylwia Denko, third grade teacher

"*Instant Relevance* offers all educators the perfect opportunity to rethink the way education is conceived. Time and time again, we hear from learners who tell us how uninspiring education is today. The techniques Sheeran outlines in this book provide a framework for bringing authenticity into the classroom. Students will be able to make connections to themselves and to the world around them, and this will naturally begin meaningful dialogue that relates to their life experiences and the real-world—giving each and every one of them a voice—inevitably leading to a higher level of engagement.

"*Instant Relevance* proves that meaning and learning can coexist in a powerful way. It provides a valuable framework that ensures that our students are reaching necessary benchmarks. Sheeran has crafted a must-read for all educators who are achieving learning outcomes by making emotional connections with curricular content.

"Do you want what your students learn to resonate with concepts, beyond just the time they spend in class with you? Do you want to bring authenticity into your classroom that gives your content context and meaning? *Instant Relevance* offers strategies that allow students to make meaningful connections between your curriculum and the real world."

—Laura Fleming, author of *Worlds of Making*

"The teachable moments that are the most memorable often aren't pulled from textbooks or old teaching materials. They're found in our everyday lives—from TV, social media, and pop culture. They're the things we—and our students—bump into every day. Denis Sheeran provides key guidance on making the most of these experiences to engage and equip students. When we aren't focused on being relevant to our students' lives, we become less and less valuable to them. This book provides practical ideas you can use in class tomorrow to bring instant relevance to your teaching.

—**Matt Miller, Google Certified Innovator, speaker,**
and author of *Ditch That Textbook*

"A natural extension of the PIRATE books and a must-read for any educator in need of revamping and sprucing up his or her teaching! There isn't a single page of this book that I haven't earmarked, highlighted, or covered in notes. I loved every single idea and suggestion from front to back cover. Denis's examples are funny, relatable, and refreshing, regardless of teaching experience. He inspired me to approach the upcoming school year on a completely different level, in which I will pay careful attention to the needs, wants, and interests of *every* single student who steps into my classroom. I absolutely loved this book, and I am so proud of Denis!

"Denis has truly captured the art of relevant teaching through the lens of the student and passion-driven classroom. His anecdotes and examples are timely, witty, and relevant to all cohorts of educators. Whether you are a student teacher or days away from retirement, *Instant Relevance* serves as an invigorating guide for individualizing teaching to create a cohesive and collaborative classroom environment."

—**Dani Kennis, high school Special Education/Social Studies**
teacher and technology coach

Instant Relevance

Using Today's Experiences to Teach Tomorrow's Lessons

Denis Sheeran

Instant Relevance

> This book is available at special discounts when purchased in quantity for use as premiums, promotions, fundraisers, or for educational use. For inquiries and details, contact the publisher at shelley@daveburgessconsulting.com.

Google and the Google logo are registered trademarks of Google Inc., images used with permission.
Typeface image used with permission under Creative Commons, Author Garethwalt.
Alexander Calder Mobile, used with permission: Alexander Calder Foundation and the Artists Rights Society.
Desmos images used with permission of Desmos.com.

Published by Dave Burgess Consulting, Inc.
San Diego, CA
http://daveburgessconsulting.com

Cover Design by Genesis Kohler
Editing and Interior Design by My Writers' Connection

Library of Congress Control Number: 2016948032
Paperback ISBN: 978-0-9969895-9-6
eBook ISBN: 978-0-9969896-0-2

First Printing: August 2016

I exist in a perpetual creative response to whatever is present.

—*Yogi Amrit Desai*

Contents

Introduction

On Sunday, February 3, 2013, I joined the tens of millions of other Americans watching the Baltimore Ravens hand the San Francisco 49ers their first Super Bowl loss in franchise history. As life would have it, I'm also one of the 58 million Americans[1] who abandoned paying for cable television in favor of not taking out a second mortgage on my house. So I watched the big game on my computer, thanks to CBS live streaming the event for free.

For many of us, one of the best parts of Super Bowl Sunday is watching the commercials. They are funny (sometimes), emotional (sometimes), inspirational (sometimes), terrible (most times), and no matter your view on them, always part of the Super Bowl experience. We all talk about which commercials we liked and disliked at work on Monday. Unfortunately, for those of us who watched Super Bowl XLVII on the Internet, CBS only aired a few commercials—repeatedly. Normally, this would get a little under my skin because to watch the good commercials online, I'd have to go to the intense trouble of opening another whole browser tab. But this year, I noticed something that disturbed me.

---

1   Based on census data of adults over eighteen (https://www.census.gov/quickfacts/table/PST045215/00) and Pew research on cord cutters (http://www.pewinternet.org/2015/12/21/4-one-in-seven-americans-are-television-cord-cutters/).

One of the commercials that had been playing again and again (which I dubbed "ad" nauseam) caught my attention, not because it was flashy and fun and sold me on the product, but because I'm a statistics teacher, and it made my data analysis alarm go off. It was the Prudential Stickers commercial. Maybe you remember it: The distinguished, yet casual, older male spokesperson asks, "What age is the oldest person you've known?"[2] The Texas residents answer by writing the person's name on a blue sticker and then put the sticker on a giant wall. **Here** was the result:

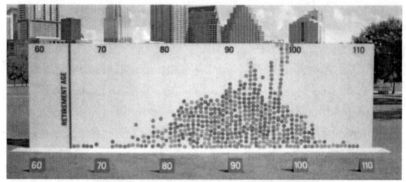

Prudential television advertisement:
"The Prudential Action Gap Experiment"

Consider my mathematical hackles raised.

You see, Prudential was trying to convince Americans that because they were likely to live well past the retirement age they should use any combination of Prudential's products to invest in and provide for their retirement. The thing is, it's not a graph of normal people; this is a graph of outliers, of the oldest people that the participants had ever known. Prudential was pulling a fast one on the public by repeatedly airing the commercial to make a lasting impression on Internet-watching casual football fans, who, coincidentally, are also very likely young and interested in investing for their retirement.

2   Prudential - Behind the Scenes at the Sticker Experiment," YouTube video, 1:30, Posted by Prudential Insurance, January 29, 2013, https://www. youtube.com/watch?v=IsNiKGMSHUQ

At that moment, I had a choice: I could either go to school the next day and rant about how false this commercial was to my math department colleagues, or I could bring the advertisement—one that most, if not all, of my students had seen less than twelve hours earlier—into my classroom and teach with it. I chose the latter. Since it was available online, I showed my advanced placement statistics students the commercial and had them think about it. Eventually, they got the sense that something didn't quite add up. Like me, they recognized Prudential was showing outliers. So I had my students pull out their Chromebooks, find data on Americans' average lifespan, and use the values on the sticker chart to create a confidence interval for the true life expectancy of Americans based on the Prudential data. The results showed people need not fear a life of penniless retirement because, sadly, they actually are much less likely to live as long as the commercial said they would. (This clearly doesn't apply to you, though. You'll live to be at least 115—I promise. If you don't, contact me and let me know.)

My students said they had never had a teacher take something they had seen just hours ago and turn it into an effective, instantly relevant learning experience (I'm paraphrasing). That's why I've titled this book: *Instant Relevance: Using Today's Experiences to Teach Tomorrow's Lessons.*

I've been teaching math at the high school and college levels since 1999, so you'll find that I've framed many of the stories in this book around my experiences in math classrooms. However, those experiences transcend content area, and I hope they will lead you to an awareness of how to connect your own experiences to your teaching. Every day, I find myself turning more and more of my experiences into opportunities that I can take to class tomorrow and turn into meaningful lessons for my students.

Let's enter that mindset together. I'll share how *Instant Relevance* can transform your classroom and help you create schools where the question "When will I use this in real life?" is never uttered again.

INSTANT

Infusing Who You Are in What You Do

Education is not preparation for life. Education is life itself.

—*John Dewey*

We've all heard about maintaining a work-life balance, but as teachers, we need to infuse our lives into our work. After all, we are teachers of people—*real* people—and through my experiences, I've learned that we can only achieve work-life balance when we bring our lives into our work, not when we separate the two.

In this chapter, we'll look at how opening ourselves up to our students helps them share in our experience, resulting in lasting connections to the content and a sense of true relevance.

Every Good Boy Deserves ...

I was talking with my wife the other day, something I get to do occasionally when our children aren't within forty feet of us. (If they're any closer, we can't hear each other. In fact, I'm fully convinced that the emotional closeness of spouses is inversely proportional to the distance between them and their kids [a mathematical study is in progress].) She's a music teacher and sings with our local oratorio society. They're doing the Beethoven Mass, and she told me her part was "difficult because of the high tessitura," which she explained as the main range of a voice part in a particular piece of music. (I minored in music in college, meaning I forgot what a tessitura is.)

To me that sounded kind of like a tessitura was the average of a musical piece for each performer. Musical average? Sounds like math to me. So I've been thinking about it, and according to *Encyclopædia Britannica* (Brittanica.com), a tessitura is "the general range of pitches found in a melody or vocal part." It differs from the compass of a piece to the extent that it does not take into account the extremes of the piece's range but is concerned with the way in which the vocal line is arranged or situated. The tessitura of a piece, therefore, is not determined by a few isolated notes of extraordinarily high or low pitch but rather by which part of the range is most consistently used.

But even beyond math, this definition got me to thinking about teaching in general. I think we, as teachers, tend to develop an "educational tessitura"—or a range of instructional styles, lesson plans, content choices, projects, and assessments—that we're comfortable with and live within. As *Encyclopædia Britannica* states, this is the range of skills we most consistently use. However, surrounding our tessitura are also a full range of other educational experiences. Some of us live within a high-energy tessitura, while others stay within more comfortable traditions. For example, when we listen to music, we appreciate

Some of us live within a high-energy tessitura, while others stay within more comfortable traditions.

each musician's skills as well as the full range of the music we hear.

For most of us, though, what lies beyond our teaching tessitura is life itself—our hobbies, our families, our struggles, our interests, the games we play, the bills we pay, the scents we prefer, and so on. Don't leave these things at the door when you walk into your classroom; bring them with you. By doing so, you'll be bringing in the unexpected possibilities and connections your students need.

———— Thinking Questions ————

1. How would you describe your "educational tessitura"? Where is your teaching range?

2. Do your students know what to expect every single day?

3. What lies outside your tessitura that could increase and beautify your work?

Work-Life Balance

We all have that one little naughty pleasure that, if anyone knew about, we'd have to find some way to quickly explain it—like a love of eating ice cream for breakfast, which we rationalize as an "overnight lactose deficiency," or the need to instantly put on barbershop quartet music as soon as we get in the car (guilty as charged). For me, and I'm not ashamed to admit this, I can't fall asleep at night unless I'm watching an episode of *Antiques Roadshow* (Now that it's out in the open, I can let the healing begin). I've watched every episode multiple times, and I've learned more about pottery and militaria than I ever thought possible. In fact, I consider myself quite the treasure hunter and have bought and sold many items for a nice little profit, but that's a story for my other book, *How to Become a Thousandaire in Eighteen Short Months*. Although I am technically capable of falling asleep without the show, I do enjoy learning from it and winding down to the ambient background noise of history slamming into treasure hunting.

While watching the show one evening, a segment came on about a hanging mobile that a woman had brought in for evaluation. It was quite small and didn't look like much, but it was wonderfully in balance and captivating in its simplicity.

Alexander Calder Mobile

The expert told the woman it was made by Alexander Calder, an artist known as the father of the mobile. I'd heard Calder's name before and knew his mobiles were considered some of the most valuable pieces of mid-century art in the world, so I continued watching. Turns out, the final appraisal for this twenty-four-inch sheet metal mobile was between $600,000 and $1 million! Needless to say, I'm now on a hunt for a forgotten Calder mobile, as my teacher's pension may not live up to its promise.

This appraisal might have easily slipped into the category of "things that help me fall asleep," had it not been for a meeting I had with a teacher the next day. He was teaching a physics lesson on center of gravity and was bouncing some ideas off me. He planned to use the meter sticks and weights to show his students that a small weight away from the center of the stick will balance against a heavy weight toward the center on the opposite side when a fulcrum is placed off-center.

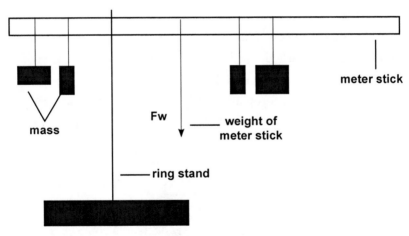

Physics-Type Apparatus

As we talked, the episode jumped into my mind—the Calder mobile was a pure, artistic example of the center of gravity concept. So I pulled up the clip online and showed him. His wonderful reaction was reflective of a good teacher: "I'd never have thought to use something like this in physics class," he told me, "but now I can't teach the lesson without it."

The night before the center of gravity lab, he had his students watch the video clip and research Calder so they could come to class ready to discuss what they had learned. He told me later that the lively discussion in class that day, along with the practical lab during which students balanced forces, directly connected them to the physics they were studying—in other words, the lesson was *real*! In fact, one of his students suggested that after each group made different balanced meter sticks, they try to stack them to make a "mobile tower," instead of a hanging one. This was a great application and idea that never would have come about if the teacher had not connected his physics lesson to art and history.

Sometimes we know what our next lesson will be, and we intentionally look for real-life connections to our material. Other times, our lessons bring our interests to light. The more you make both types of connections, the more you'll naturally recognize moments that you can use immediately in your lessons to *generate instant relevance*.

Thinking Questions

1. Which of your hobbies or guilty pleasures could be a great opportunity to connect your students with your content?

2. When you hear your colleagues talking about lessons and a connection comes to mind, do you share it? What would happen if you did?

Why My Students Care About My Lunch

I like to eat. For me, eating regularly battles for the top spot on the list of things needed to survive—sometimes losing out to sleep and occasionally to a fresh cup of coffee. But as you most likely know, not all foods are created equal, and some could even be considered abominations of nature. So one day, when I was sitting in the kitchen with my wife—wondering why our kids were nowhere to be found and what it was going to cost us once we found them—out of the blue, she said, "Hey, do you remember those Hostess apple pies? The ones you get at gas stations? I always wanted those as a kid." I instantly pictured the headline: "Man Divorces Wife Over Unhealthy Pie Preference." After realizing divorce probably wasn't the best option, something else came to mind, and I replied, "That 'food' is not worth eating—but it *is* worth graphing!"

So I took my nerdery to the best place to graph things you wouldn't expect to graph: the online calculator at Desmos.com.

Here's the result:

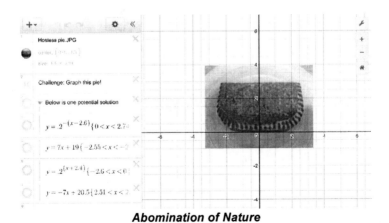

Abomination of Nature

Here's where Instant Relevance kicked in. I've done things like this in the past—Tweeting graphs of food or trees or other graphable things to my math friends for their approval and sometimes just taking pleasure in living up to my own graphical expectations for myself. This time, though, I took the graphing challenge to my students. I told them about my wife and her therapy-inducing desire for that aforementioned food product and then sent them the link to the pie graph (pun intended) with two challenges: First, graph the pie. Second, graph the pie using the fewest number of functions possible.

They loved it. (The graphing, not the pie—no one likes those pies. That's why they have indefinite expiration dates.) The best part, though, was the next day when my students came to class asking, "What food are we graphing today?" I hadn't expected this, so I ran to my office and grabbed the slice of leftover pizza I'd brought for my lunch. I took a picture of it, uploaded the photo to Desmos.com, and set them to task. I ate my lunch while they came up with this:

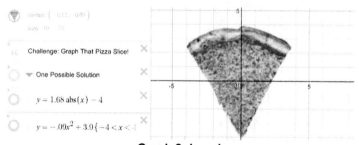

Graph 2: Lunch

The rest of the school year the question, "Mr. Sheeran, what do you have for lunch?" was much more than small talk—it meant a connection to learning. My students knew I'd bring food that I didn't even like, just so they could graph it. We didn't do this every day. We did have other topics to talk about that graphing wasn't a part of, but I secretly hoped they were starting to see the things around them the way I did— as opportunities for graphing, investigating, and learning.

Turns out, they were. I started receiving e-mails with links to graphed hamburgers, tomatoes, candy, vegetables, and more. Then, one day, I sat down to dinner and there it was, staring at me. In nine to twelve minutes, over medium-high heat, my wife had prepared the most difficult math graphing task I've ever encountered: cavatappi pasta.

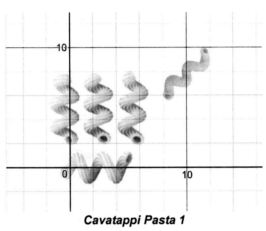

Cavatappi Pasta 1

It was actually pretty easy to use trigonometry to hit the curves. (See, trig *can* be useful!)

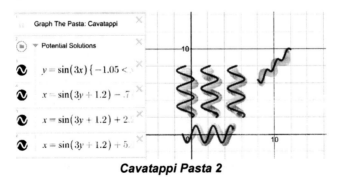

Cavatappi Pasta 2

Then I asked my students to take on the bigger challenge: to graph the tube itself. *How do you graph a tube?* It became such a huge task that it took the rest of the year for them to realize something very difficult:

they just couldn't do it. But instead of giving up, we asked Desmos's founder and CEO, Eli Luberoff, and his team if they could help. One of the most important things a student can learn in their school career is that they are not intended or expected to be masters of everything, and *sometimes* it's best to ask someone who knows more than you do. This was one of those moments, and, amazingly, Eli and the Desmos team came through with this amazing creation:

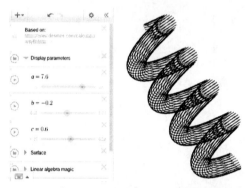

Cavatappi Pasta Awesome

A simple, easy-to-make dinner became a challenge too big for my students to accomplish alone then transformed into one of the most important lessons they'll ever learn: accept challenges, persist, ask for help, and learn.

Thinking Questions

1. When a small idea grows too big to handle, do you abandon it or do you find help?

2. Do you have any ideas that you've abandoned that you'd like to revive?

3. What everyday needs, like eating, can you use to connect your lessons to your students?

Bringing Your Life into the Classroom

Every spring, school districts across the country see a shift in their staff. Some teachers retire or resign, and new positions are created and filled. As a mathematics supervisor for an entire school district, I have the privilege of interviewing many of the candidates applying for these open positions.

After the slew of standard interview questions about the candidate's background and experiences, I like to shift the interview and tell this story:

It was the summer of 2001. I was twenty-five, I had just broken up with my girlfriend "for good," and the last of my friends from college had just walked for his degree. Before jobs and lives got in our way, a couple of buddies and I decided to travel to Europe together as part of a church choir and orchestra trip. We would spend three weeks touring England and Scotland, performing in churches, then add on three more weeks to visit Paris, Spain, Italy, Austria, and Germany on our own.

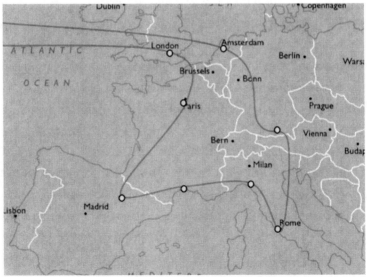

Indiana Jones-Style Travel Map

A major stop on our trip was in Pamplona, Spain, to participate in the San Fermin Festival's annual Running of the Bulls. We arrived in Pamplona the night before the festival started, only to find that our hotel had been triple-booked. And since we had shown up third, we got to spend the night in our rental car, which, thankfully, had been upgraded to a minivan. (That's right, I drove around Europe in a minivan, and I'd do it again.) Since we didn't have a hotel to crash in, we bought some scalped tickets to the evening's bullfight so we could witness a great cultural event.

The next morning, my friends backed out of running. They were scared, or something like that, as if bulls that had been penned up for a while get aggressive. I decided I would still run. After packing myself into the human pen with 300 other people (of which approximately 94 percent were Americans between the ages of twenty and twenty-seven), we heard a gunshot signaling that our gates were opening and we could begin the 800-meter run to the bullfighting arena. About a minute later, after I'd barely started moving with the crowd, we heard a second gunshot letting us know that the bulls had been released into the streets.

I kept jogging down the road, as if nothing were happening, because it felt like nothing was happening. Then, suddenly, the sound changed. The tapping of rubber-soled athletic shoes was overpowered by the thunderous pounding of the eight 1,500-pound animals charging at us, shaking the street. I had about a hundred meters left to run, so I took off, easily breaking the world record for the hundred-meter dash (thanks, in part, to the wind). As I approached the arena's arched entryway, a man tripped and fell. I went into full track-and-field mode, hurdling over him with what felt like spectacular form (but from the sidelines, was probably a bit less spectacular), all the while forgetting I was supposed to run toward the side when I entered the arena. So I ran straight out into the middle. I looked behind me, and three feet away was the first bull, charging toward me. I pivoted to the right. His nose caught the back of my foot. I fell, scraped my knee on the arena's bloodied gravel, and then ran for the wall as the bull tried to slow his momentum and turn after me. As I made it over the wall and reached safety, I muttered "thank you" to the sky.

Entering the Arena

Scraped, but Safe, after the Run

What I didn't know was that behind me, on the street, a twenty-five-year-old—also from New Jersey—had been nearly gored to death. My ex-girlfriend, who knew I was running, heard the news and proceeded to e-mail me more than a hundred times over the course of two days to make sure I wasn't dead. When I finally reached an Internet cafe and responded, we both realized that "for good" should become "for better or for worse" instead. She's now my wife of thirteen years.

At this point in the interview, I always pause and say, "When I'm asked, 'What's the most interesting thing that's ever happened to you?' I reply with that story. What's your answer?"

At first, I'm usually met with befuddled silence, but it doesn't take long for the candidate to get personal and begin sharing their story, pouring out their passion about a life experience. I then ask, "Now, how will you use that story, and stories like it, in your classroom?"

That's when I learn the most about them.

Similarly, sharing stories in class opens the door, even floodgates, for our students to learn about us and become comfortable talking about their own life experiences, which you can then use in your teaching. This is the biggest learning pyramid scheme out there. Your story can lead to a few more from students, then more students are willing to share, until you've got more experiences and moments collected than you know what to do with. When you tap into your students' lives, your class immediately becomes relevant. So share your stories, even if they don't teach a standard or a lesson, and before you know it, your students will start offering their stories as resources as well. Keep a journal of their ideas, and when the time is right, have students share a story that connects to the class that day.

Thinking Questions

1. What stories and experiences came to mind when you read, "What's yours?"

2. How will you integrate those stories and others like them into your classroom experience?

INSTANT

Natural Flow:
Follow the Question

We live in the worlds our questions create.

—Dr. David Cooperrider

As a youngster growing up in the 1980s, one of the movies I watched multiple times—both for entertainment and curious inspiration—was *The Goonies*. If you've never seen this movie, I'm sure there's a copy available at your local library or in an oversized three-dollar DVD bin at your local gas station. What I still like about *The Goonies* is that the kids, hunting for the treasure of the pirate, One-Eyed Willy, have no idea what awaits them around the next corner. They end up in places and see things they never expected to see or experience.

As I reflect on many moments from my teaching, I realize I lost out on opportunities to learn unexpectedly because I stopped the momentum of a question in its tracks. Maybe the question was my own, or maybe a student asked it, but I was so caught up in my plans for the day that I couldn't divert. I wonder now what amazing new ideas I would have experienced if I had allowed the questions to take me to unexpected places back then. This chapter includes examples of times where I followed the natural flow of a question to exciting, unexpected, and relevant learning experiences.

Unanswerable Questions

Has this ever happened to you? You pull into your garage or drive-way after a long day at work and thought, *wow, I don't even remember driving home!* If I'm the only person who ever does this, I recommend you stay off Route 80 West in New Jersey between four and five o'clock on weekdays for your own safety. The reality of the situation, though, is that we spend a significant portion of our daily lives completely unaware of our surroundings, completely missing out on countless opportunities to connect our personal lives to our teaching.

I've started seeing the things around me, even the smallest ones, as possible lesson activities, essential questions, and classroom openers. For example, one day I was looking up something on Google (as I'm frequently known to do) when Google finished my search request for me, not unlike this generic version of that moment:

Google Search of Google Searches

At that moment, I realized I could ask Google part of a question then take its suggestion and go down a road filled with inquiry and discovery. Better yet, I could use Google's suggested questions to engage my students at the start of class. I was tired of the traditional "do now" problem class opener, or posting a practice problem from the previous night's homework for students to work on, while I walked around checking homework. If that last sentence made you want to pass out in your chair, then you had the same response my math class students did when I, unfortunately, had them complete "do now" problems each day. What's more, the students who'd done well on the homework and understood yesterday's lesson would sit there, waiting for their peers to finish. This was an amazing waste of learning time.

Now enter my realization that Google asks great questions. In fact, I deem many of the questions that Google uses to fill my search starters "Unanswerable Questions."

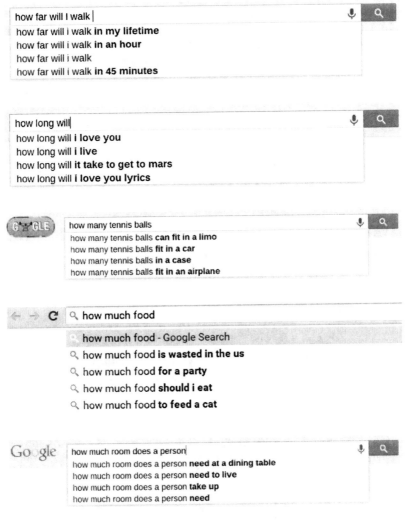

So Many Unanswerable Questions

In each of these question sets, I let my students choose which one we answer as a class. At the start of the period, students take out their computers or phones and begin researching the question's answer. They spend a few minutes deciding how to answer, determine which information to use, and do some calculations before I finally have them share their answer with a partner and report to the class. The whole process takes about seven minutes, but each and every student engages in mathematical thinking. Even if the question has nothing to do with the day's lesson, the students prepare their minds to look at a situation critically, identify variables, use appropriate tools for calculations, engage in mathematical discourse, and communicate their decisions to a group. Later in the class, when I pose a situation involving parabolas or trigonometry, their responses are similar to how they responded to the Unanswerable Question. I forever changed my class by using these questions daily to transform their "do now time" into "think now time."

And this is just the start. Too often, we place the lesson plan's importance over the value of our students' experience. We must prepare ourselves to follow a question down an unexpected road at any point. We are the content experts in the room, after all, and as such, we should use our knowledge to guide our students to understanding—not force them into compliance. That's why, when you hear a question you didn't expect, I encourage you to follow it down that unknown path, to see where it leads, and to then connect it all back together. Most of the

We must prepare ourselves to follow a question down an unexpected road at any point.

friends in *The Goonies* didn't believe that the treasure of One-Eyed Willy existed. But by following one who believed, they ended up being changed by the experience. (They also ended up with a marble sack full of comically large jewels). Take the first step and see where your classroom treasure map leads.

Sweethearts

I have four children with my first wife (She's still my first wife, and she doesn't really like it when I call her that, especially in print.). One day, my second-oldest child, who is in the fourth grade, brought home a letter about her class's upcoming Valentine's Day party. I, ever the school-party skeptic, was curious about the educational value of a Valentine's Day party, so I read the letter hoping to find out. After reading through the list of my daughter's classmates' first names, I came to a note at the bottom stating:

We will be making Valentine's Day mailboxes in class on Friday. As discussed in class, we are also exchanging valentines (no food allowed). All students are expected to participate and must bring in one valentine for every other student in the class.

This sent my wife and me down a discussion path for a few minutes that included such topics as "Why are they forcing foodless romance on nine-year-olds?" or "What happens if she's giving up Valentine's Day for Lent?" and "Are they at least learning geometry while making the mailboxes?"

And since most store-bought "nutrition-free" valentines aren't much fun, my daughter and I made our own for her to pass out.

Our Delicious Valentine

While we were making and filling out her valentines, she was eating those little conversation hearts. I could tell she was eating them because of the jackhammer sound her orthodontic work was making as she chewed them. She even admitted that she didn't really like them but was eating them because they are candy and, well, she's a kid. It seems my nine-year-old has reached self-actualization a lot faster than I did. Without even realizing it, I asked her a math question: "Since you don't really like them, and no one really does, what if we took all the conversation hearts made this year and stacked them up. Do you think the stack would reach the moon?"

When she finished filling out her last bacon valentine, we decided to look into my question. A quick Internet search provided us with the basics.

Sweethearts are made by the New England Confectionery Company, or Necco. A similar type of candy is sold in the UK under the name Love Hearts. Necco manufactures nearly **8 billion Sweethearts** per year.

Only 8 Billion?

238,900 miles
(384,400 km)

Moon, Distance to Earth

Moon, Distance from Earth

We then set to work, converting miles into feet and feet into inches. She got stuck trying to look up how big a candy heart was in inches. That's when I reminded her of a very interesting math trick I learned at her age: actually measuring. Turns out, candy hearts are a half-inch across. All the math worked out to the hearts reaching a mere 63,131 miles. Love is in the air, albeit really, really far up in the air. But not quite to the moon.

That night, I e-mailed her teacher to let her know what we'd done and how much my daughter had enjoyed the process. She was fully engaged in the context of the problem from start to finish without me once telling her she was doing a (deep breath) *word problem*. In fact, she didn't even seem to notice. Her teacher thought the exercise was a great way to connect the party to their math content, so she used it as well and gave students this very cool homework assignment:

"Since we didn't reach the moon, choose a direction from here to wrap your candy heart stack around the world and come in tomorrow to let us know where you can send a message."

My daughter and I had so much fun hypothetically sending messages all over the world that we decided to actually send a valentine to Burkina Faso, one of the places we'd landed. We mailed "Luv U" to the American embassy there, which also happens to have one of my favorite addresses of all time: Ouaga 2000, Ouagadougou, Burkina Faso. I don't know if the embassy got the heart or if it got cut off in customs, but we never would have had the idea had my daughter's teacher not used her own creativity to expand upon a parent's idea.

Thinking Questions

1. How could you enrich your students' annual rituals by connecting them to a content-related activity?

2. Have you dismissed parents who've offered suggestions, or have you embraced their ideas as potential opportunities?

3. How can you give your students' parents a voice in sharing content ideas while retaining your leadership role?

Meet Me at My Best

My kids and I play a game called Ball Jump on my iPhone and iPad. It's a lot of stressful fun. As you jump from block formation to block formation, the formations change shape and orientation right under you. I have a math activity in progress involving this game (of course I do).

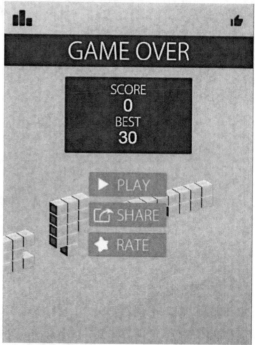

Ridiculously Addicting Game

My four-year-old son has gotten pretty good at the game. In fact, he's really good—he has a higher record score than my nine-year-old daughter. Recently, he wanted me to play Ball Jump on my iPhone while he played it on our iPad so we could "meet" in the game. And while it was more of a Minecraft-implanted idea than one of pure father-son sweetness and familial connections, it wasn't the idea of meeting in the game that has stayed with me—it was how he said it: "Meet me at my best, Dad. Then we can go together."

In my opinion, there is no better way to describe the teacher-student relationship, the administrator-teacher relationship, and the connections we form each day than in the words: "Meet me at my best. Then we can go together."

Every day, students land in our classrooms, coming from different places with different abilities, problems, and talents. Each day, they grow at different rates, learning and mastering content in different ways. I encourage you to meet your students at their best and then go together from there. Their backgrounds, their levels of understanding, and their questions create the natural tides and currents that will power your class.

In the words of the late Lao Tzu: "Life is a series of natural and spontaneous changes. Don't resist them—that only creates sorrow. Let reality be reality. Let things flow naturally forward in whatever way they like."

INSTANT

Sudden Changes
to Your Surroundings

*Perhaps it's the people whose lives have taken sudden
new twists—people who have learned to embrace the
creative possibilities of change—who stand the best
chance of penetrating life's mysteries.*

—*Hugh Mackay*

Our minds and bodies thrive on routine. We have routines for eating, sleeping, washing, driving, and just about everything. When a sudden event throws off our routine, our bodies and minds often react with disdain for that event or the person who caused it. However, sudden and unexpected changes to your surroundings or environment are also frequently a shared experience. When the power goes out at school, the students, teachers, and administration all experience it. When a teacher has a baby, the students celebrate. When a district decides to go to a 1:1 technology model, we must all react together and embrace the change. Here are two stories—one from the surface and one that shook my foundation—that I hope will encourage you to embrace sudden changes as vehicles for creating relevance to your students' learning experience.

'That's a Ton of Snow!'

Last winter, I was in the middle of removing what would be the last snowfall of the season when my Toro CR-20 snow blower decided to seize, fill my lungs with exhaust, quit, and never start again. At the time, I didn't bother giving it a proper burial, nor did I bother replacing it. What I did do was procrastinate in replacing it for so long that when the next season's first snow landed in my driveway, I realized that yesterday would have been a great day to contact the guy on Craigslist selling the updated model, the Toro CCR-2000E. Instead of going back in time, I grabbed my shovel, went outside, and set to clearing my driveway.

Not a Bad Job, if I Say So Myself

While I was outside, it seems my eleven-year-old daughter had told my wife, "There's a *ton of snow* in the driveway!" So when I came in the house, I could hear my wife describing the concept of a hyperbole to her. I gave my wife the "Oh, it's *not* a ton of snow, is it? My lower back respectfully disagrees" look (You know the one.) and suggested that my daughter either back up her claim or retract her statement with a formal written apology. After all, this was the perfect time for a language lesson on exaggerated statements not meant to be taken seriously—or was it?

What happened next is truly the model for *Instant Relevance*. My daughter asked me how much snow was out there, so I showed her the photo I'd taken for Facebook to share my experience with friends.

Fresh Powder

My daughter then asked how big the driveway was, so I handed her the measuring tape and her boots, and I waited. When she came back with the measurements, we drew a map of the driveway.

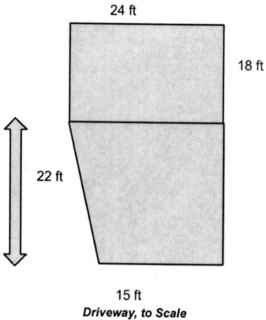

Driveway, to Scale

She then took out a formula sheet (an available resource), and we found the volume of the prism the eight inches of snow had made in the driveway. Then she spent some time correcting her answer because she'd forgotten to convert the eight inches of snow to feet (kids these days). After she showed me her final answer, I asked for her written apology. Once her confusion subsided and it finally hit her, she said, "Oh, yeah, the weight. How heavy is snow?"

I'd like to thank the USDA for the invaluable information on its website. With its help, we learned that in our region of the country, during the two-week period of winter we were in, snow is typically 20 percent water. A few conversions later, my daughter had found that I'd moved 114.8 cubic feet of water, and that one cubic foot of water weighs 62.42796 pounds, so I'd actually moved 7,167 pounds, or 3.5835 tons of snow.

My wife's formal apology to my daughter is now on the fridge.

That day, my conversation turned from annoyance with a snow blower to a language lesson, then to a challenge, next a measurement, a calculation, a conversion, a comparison, a communication, a clarification, an apology, and finally a connection. Not once did my daughter ever act as if she was spending her time *learning*.

Not once did my daughter ever act as if she was spending her time learning.

The next day, I went to school and shared my experience with a group of seventh-grade teachers. After the other teachers left the room, one asked, "Can I have the pictures? I'd love to ask my third-period class this question." She was the last teacher to leave the room, and the only one to ask for the pictures. But I could tell she was focused on connecting her lesson to what her students might care about. The other teachers gave their classes a practice packet on fraction conversion that day. If students had talked about their math class at lunch that day (which, who am I kidding, of course they do), I wonder who said, "Math class was really interesting today."

———— Thinking Questions ————

1. Have you or your family ever made a claim at home that could lead to learning in your classroom? What type of lesson could you build around that claim?

2. How could the weather play a role in your lesson plans? Do you have any stories about an experience you had with the weather that can hook your students into the lesson?

Shaking the Foundation

It's so important not to underestimate even your smallest ideas—while they may only be sparks for you, they could light a fire under one of your students and eventually become a flame for change. When you discover that a student or a group of students cares about a connection you used in class, something special happens.

Case in point: A teacher who inspires me, Jennifer Gonzales (cultofpedagogy.com) wrote a blog post about a change to a practice I'd been taught in my sophomore year of high school. I'd even argued with people about this practice and thought, "They must be wrong—this is what I learned!" What could be so emotionally important, so set in stone, that I would stick to my guns at all costs? It was this cornerstone belief: When typing, place two spaces after a period.

No Way! I'm sure you agree this is monumentally important and worth losing friends over. But it wasn't until I read the blog post that I learned including two spaces is no longer standard. It is, indeed, one space only. That's because digital typing accommodates for the letters' size and, as such, uses less space for narrow letters and more for wider ones, making the spacebar space the largest overall. This is known as "proportional type." Typewriters and fancy-schmancy Brother word processors used a system called "monotype," where the spacebar and every letter took up the same (mono) amount of space on the paper. Larger words in proportional type take up the same space as smaller ones in monotype. See what I mean?

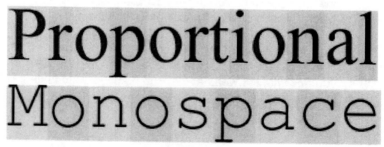

Typeface Differences

Now I hope you've enjoyed the history lesson because it's over. As I read this, the question that came to my mind, and then to my mouth, was, "How much paper have we wasted just because we didn't know this rule?"

And there it was: the connection I needed. So I began working on a lesson that would have students finding text online (which uses one space) and editing it so that it has two spaces after the period. They would then measure the excess printing and project outward, using only teachers in the United States (most likely to not know the rule). It turns out that, annually, we teachers print more than 535 million excess pages! I had a good time working this problem through with my students, and at the end, we were all amazed and thinking *mathally* (it's a word) about how much space the wasted paper would fill up.

I didn't know it, but at the time, three of my students were very passionate about environmental conservation. I knew, from daily experience, that they recycled everything, which many students do, and occasionally noticed that one was very adept at reusing materials instead of wasting them. (He'd bring his lunch in an empty bread bag and his milk in an empty soda bottle and, after he was done, tuck everything away to take home and use again.) But that day, my lesson brought about more than *mathal* (it's a word) amazement—it brought about action.

Those three students decided it was time to do something about the excess paper use we'd discovered, so they researched its economic and environmental impacts, presented their findings to the school's environmental club, and started a campaign to educate teachers in the area and schools around the state about how to cut back on their paper use by "conserving spaces."

I've found that when students care, students act. By making students think about something so everyday that it's almost second nature, like the spacing after a period, we can positively affect the environment in both the short and long term.

When students care, students act.

The most powerful weapon on earth is the human soul on fire.

—*Ferdinand Foch*

—————— Thinking Questions ——————

1. Which of your longstanding beliefs could be impeding your growth as a teacher? How can embracing a necessary change affect your students' learning and lives for the better?

2. When change is necessary, do you think about what is being lost by the change, or do you consider what is being gained? What are the benefits of viewing the future effects of change?

INSTANT

Television and Pop Culture

Popular culture is where the pedagogy is,
it's where the learning is.

—bell hooks

Pop culture and television references are part of our daily lives, and they provide us remarkable ways to connect with our students and make the content we teach relevant. You might be surprised to find how many of your students watch the same shows as you, listen to the same music you do, and vote for the same contestant on *The Voice* as you did (standard messaging rates may apply).

Television and pop culture inspire my lessons, help me connect with my students, and spark curiosity in more ways than I can share here. As you read about my experiences, your own pop culture and television references will probably start coming to mind—use them. Find and reveal your stories to your students so you, too, can forge connections and discover Instant Relevance.

A Moment of Inspiration, from the Good People at Apple

My wife and I like the music of Pink Floyd. My wife is a bigger fan of the band's singer, songwriter, and guitarist, David Gilmour, than I am, but I like his music. Since we were lucky enough to have gotten tickets to his April show at Madison Square Garden, I preordered his new album, *Rattle That Lock*, on iTunes. Apple had been releasing singles from the album occasionally to drive interest, as they're known to do, and a few months prior to his concert, I received the e-mail below announcing the release of the next song.

iTunes Store: "Today" is now available. ⚑

iTunes Store to you   show details ⌄

iTunes E-mail of Song Release

While "Today" is just the next song on *Rattle That Lock*, and I was excited to hear it, that day Apple accidentally sent me a bigger message—one focusing on an interest in momentary awareness that comes when we connect ourselves to our surroundings: "When you wake up each day, instead of focusing on the world about to happen, focus on the fact that you've woken up, that you're breathing, and that you have today to live, moment by moment." That's an important concept for all of us.

The day I received this message, I decided to abandon my math plans. I told my students about the e-mail. I told them that we often have our heads in the past or in the future but not in the present. I let them think and talk about what was important to them. We didn't talk about math that day, but to some of the students, that was the day that life connected to learning.

Thinking Questions
---

1. Are you prepared to abandon your lesson plan for the day and replace it with an experience you feel your students need? What are the benefits of being ready to do this?

2. How do you use music in your class? What ways can you connect the music the students are listening to with your lessons and learning?

Problem Solving, Three Ways

I was doing an official observation of a third-grade math teacher's classroom and, for some reason, she was nervous. So because of her nerves, she wrote the problem of the day *and* the solution to the problem on the board. As we all know, students are notoriously good at pointing out our mistakes, so in less than a second, they began saying, "You wrote the answer, too!" This teacher, on this day, looked at her students and gave the perfect response: "The answer isn't what's important; the process and thinking you use to reach the answer are. Now, solve the problem three different ways and then share them with your partner."

Food Network Show, Chopped

This instantly reminded me of Food Network's *Chopped*, one of my favorite television shows to binge-watch on Netflix. I *do not* suggest watching Food Network shows after 9:00 p.m. because doing so leads to what I call "Dinner: The Sequel" and what doctors call "an unhealthy lifestyle." Each episode, chefs are given a basket with several seemingly unrelated ingredients. Each chef then has thirty minutes to make a top-level dinner entree to serve to professional chefs, who then judge the creations based on multiple dinner-related criteria. I actually do something similar on "leftover night" at home, only replace the professional chefs with annoyed children, who also judge the meal based on multiple dinner-related criteria.

After watching several episodes in an attempt to boost my leftover night creativity, I began to see a pattern: for many of the entrees, the chefs focus on a main ingredient and prepare it three different ways. The result is real-time problem solving.

For example, salmon three ways might consist of chipotle-roasted salmon, oven-steamed salmon with dill mayonnaise, and grilled salmon salad with potatoes. But salmon is, of course, a normal-sounding dinner ingredient, making it the type of food that would never make its way into a *Chopped* ingredient basket. So instead, the chefs might be given cold veggie pizza to prepare three ways. (Use your imagination on this one.) I suggest using eggs. I've used leftover sausage pizza, cut into small pieces, as the foundation for a baked egg casserole. You just add eggs and a little more cheese then bake it for twenty-five minutes at 375 degrees. The pizza fluffs up, absorbs the egg/cheese mixture, and is a surprisingly good breakfast. Hungry yet? I hope you're not reading this within thirty minutes of bedtime.

Afterward, the judges reward the chefs who creatively and successfully pull off a fast entree three ways by moving them on to the next round to cook again. At the end, the last chef standing wins $10,000 (My pizza egg casserole can definitely take home the big bucks.). In school, so many of us believe our students should solve problems as quickly as possible by following a single, time-tested path. Although this path may lead to a successful solution, all too often, it doesn't help the students move on to the next round of learning.

We live in a world where creativity is valued more than "the right answer," where we no longer think outside the box—we wonder why there was a box to begin with. So when you teach, allow your stu-

> *We live in a world where creativity is valued more than "the right answer."*

dents to follow the most natural route to solving a problem, whether it's mathematical or scientific or literary. Then have them talk to one another about what was natural for them. Hopefully soon, creative problem solvers will be everywhere, from famous kitchens to our own homes and everywhere in between.

Thinking Questions

1. In what other ways does the *Chopped* show act as a metaphor for teaching and learning? What other metaphors and examples of good teaching and learning are present in TV shows you watch?

2. What unexpected ingredients can you mix into your class to create a surprising and memorable outcome?

3. When a student presents an alternative idea or solution, how do you react?

One for You...

My children often ask me to watch cartoons with them. They enjoy the company, but I hate the cartoons they like, so I don't do it as often as I probably should to retain my Fun Dad badge. I was at the library one day, though, and saw a DVD of old *Looney Tunes* episodes and thought that making my kids watch the cartoons I loved as a kid would be a great way to connect. Not surprisingly, my kids didn't like the outdated and less flashy style of *Looney Tunes*. But Fun Dad had the remote, so we went on a watching spree.

An episode came on showing two mobsters hiding from the police and divvying up the money they'd stolen. The lead mobster says, "One for you," giving his crony a bill, and "One for me," giving himself one. He then says, "Two for you," giving his crony another bill, but—and here's where it gets interesting—he follows up with, "One, two for me" and gives himself two more bills. In retrospect, he *is* a thief, so I shouldn't have expected him to be honest.

At this point, one of my daughters said, "No fair! He's getting twice as much money as the other guy." Without knowing it, she had just baited the hook for a great problem on sequences and series (the sum of a sequence's terms). A few days later, I showed my class the cartoon and gave them this question: "If the mobster has $10,000 in his hand in hundred-dollar bills and keeps going this way, what will be the last amount that he hands himself?" Have fun with that one. (You can feel free to Tweet me your answers if you decide to work it out @MathDenisNJ.)

I've also already mentioned things like the Super Bowl, commercials, *Antiques Roadshow*, and a popular iPhone game before even discussing them as TV and pop culture references. They are pervasive throughout our days. I encourage you to find and reveal these references in order to connect with your students and create Instant Relevance.

Thinking Questions

1. Which television shows do both you and your students watch? How could you work at least one of those shows into a lesson to make the lesson more engaging and fun?

2. How can you use your classroom's technology to make videos like this accessible?

Down with the Sickness

Most teachers will tell you they hate being sick, not that being sick is intrinsically terrible, but because "it's more work to be out of school than it is to be there." That can be true, but sometimes you just can't help it, and you have to take a day off. I like to take advantage of my sick days and watch *The Price Is Right*. In fact, probably the only time I watch *The Price Is Right* these days is when I'm sick, nursing a ginger ale, and snacking on saltines. Game shows provide me with a wonderful opportunity to have a discussion about probability: What are the chances a contestant will win? How did the probability change after the contestant lost the first part of the game? What are the chances someone with a Flock of Seagulls haircut will be selected next?

One sick day, I was watching *The Price Is Right*, analyzing whether contestants were playing the odds correctly or using instinct (inferential statistics), and guessing who would win when I recalled a book by Dan Ariely called *Predictably Irrational*. In it, Ariely tries to understand why we make the decisions we make, even when they seem strange. For example, why do we keep buying coffee at one place when we could go to another place and pay a third of the cost? Why do we purchase subscriptions when they come with something free? At this point, I'd stopped analyzing *The Price Is Right's* games for math purposes, since the games are all pretty straightforward, and instead, shifted my thinking to how we make choices. Some contestants seemed rational, others constantly polled the audience, and still some acted like it was the first time they'd ever heard of a motorcycle.

Later that week, I shared my thoughts with a sociology professor at the community college where I teach. The central theme of the unit he was currently teaching was "Social Influence." We talked for a while about the factors that impact the decisions people make, and he left our conversation ready to ask his students questions about what they saw in *The Price Is Right* that could help them better understand people and decision making. What began as my amazement with how poorly contestants guess the price of dish soap ended with an opportunity for students, whom I may never teach, to learn more about themselves and their class content. As a side note, I also fell asleep halfway through *The Price Is* Right that day, so if you can tell me who won the Showcase Showdown on January 18, 2011, I'd appreciate it.

——————— Thinking Questions ———————

1. Whether planned or unexpected, how can you make a day when you're not in school still relevant to your students? How does your answer to that question affect your mindset toward days when you are in the classroom?

2. What's your favorite game show? How could you relate it to your students, content, and storytelling?

INSTANT
Awareness of Your Surroundings

*Awareness is like the sun. When it shines on things,
they are transformed.*

—*Thich Nhat Hanh*

Through my experiences, I've learned that by simply becoming aware of your surroundings, you can more easily see connections in the things and people around you. The initial wonderment I experienced because of these accidental *aha* moments has led me to pursue a purposeful, inquisitive hunt for more of those moments. I've actually stopped mid-walk because I saw a sign or situation that I could use in a future lesson. And I know some of this may seem overwhelming—you have a curriculum to cover, pacing guides to hold to, team teachers to work with, and more—and by no means am I suggesting you rip out the roots of learning in favor of a moment-by-moment approach. Rather, neatly tuck away the ideas and connections you make so you can access them later on, when they fit into your curriculum, and then do what every good teacher does: tell your students the story happened yesterday!

Sir Francis Bacon (from my daughter's valentine) said, "Begin doing what you want to do now. We are not living in eternity. We have only this moment, sparkling like a star in our hand—and melting like a snowflake."[1]

Running on Fumes

If I'm any good at guessing things about people, which I may or may not be, then I'm absolutely (or at least mostly) certain that you either drive or don't drive a car. Am I right? Sweet.

Driving means buying gas and, in my case, that means buying gas often, as my commute comes in at around one hundred miles daily. When I recently filled up my gas tank, I noticed both the fuel range and odometer.

Full Tank! Woohoo!

As a professional "noticer of math things," a few miles later at a stop light, I noticed the fuel range and odometer again.

---

1   Sir Francis Bacon, "Francis Bacon>Quotes>Quotable Quotes," Goodreads.com, 2016, http://www.goodreads.com/quotes/128825-begin-doing-what-you-want-to-do-now-we-are.

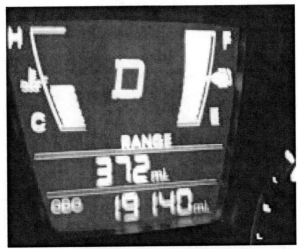

Mostly Full Tank! Woohoo!

What differences do you see? What does that make you think? Now let me show you a few more.

I drive a lot.

Over the miles I spent burning up that gas tank, I took twenty-nine photos of my odometer (not while driving, my wife would kill me). I'll spare you the rest, but I showed my students all of them because I spare them nothing. Like my students, you may have noticed that the remaining fuel range is not in sync with my odometer. But since my students are in my math class, they didn't just get to notice something; they had to make a graph.

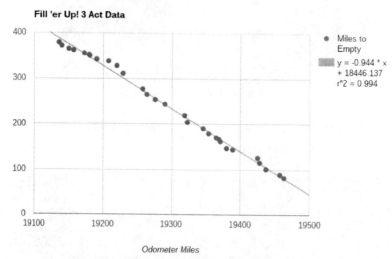

Showing Me that it's Time to Get Gas, Again

I just happened to notice the difference as I drove and, on a whim, decided to take twenty-nine photos that would lead to this lesson. The result was an opportunity for students to predict, then investigate, then analyze their prediction, and eventually come to a conclusion (Mr. Sheeran needs a hobby.).

Thinking Questions

1. How can you use your commute to engage your students?

2. When you're "running on fumes," how do you motivate yourself?

America the Beautiful

I like to talk about food. That's because nothing is more instantly relevant to both me and many of my students than the need to eat to survive. And when you think about it, food is also a pretty amazing thing. Its shapes, colors, sizes, and varieties disappear as soon as we devour it, leaving behind only crumbs of its former existence. So before you eat your next meal, I challenge you to look at and think about your food for thirty seconds. What comes to mind (besides "I'm hungry")? If you can say, "Oh, that's interesting," about the food in front of you, then take a little bit longer and figure out how to give your students the opportunity to say the same thing.

Here are two lessons taught using a birthday cake:

Lesson 1: The Math One

One of the teachers I work with has quite a happy little girl. A few days before her daughter's eighth birthday, my colleague came to me to let me know she'd be taking Friday off to bake a birthday cake. Surprised, I asked, "Really? The whole day?" She replied, "Oh, you've never seen my birthday cakes!" It turns out she was making a three-tiered cake covered in American Girl red fondant and adorned with rhinestones and stars. Check it out—it is pretty amazing.

Tiers of Love
Printed with permission from Dagmar Cordano.

The Monday after the party, she offered me a towering slice of the leftover base cake that I can only assume could be used as a flotation device in the event of a water landing. But since I always look at food with a mathematical lens, the first thing out of my mouth before the cake went into it was, "Are you going to show this picture to your geometry students? There's so much math in there!" I mean, there you have it, kids: math *from* real life! She said she was going to take the photo to class but, to my disappointment, only to show her students what she had made over the weekend. This was a major missed opportunity!

So as not to have the cake go entirely to educational waste, I decided to show the photo to my statistics students. Even though it's a wonderful model for geometry, I knew my students could learn something from it. My class reacted with *wows, oohs, ahs,* and other unprintable comments about how big it was. But then it came: the question. "That's too much frosting. I hate frosting. *How much frosting did she use?*" Bingo! Now it was time to get to work. So I asked my students to figure it out. They proceeded to ask more questions, like how tall the cake was, what the diameter of each part was, and so on. And when they needed more information, I gave it to them. But don't forget, I had actually seen this thing in person, so I got the information in advance (highly suggested teaching trick). Someone yelled, "Wait! There's frosting missing from between the two layers—take that out!" My students were doing this problem, without my prodding them to go on and finish, because they

> *My students were doing this problem, without my prodding them to go on and finish, because they wanted to.*

wanted to. They wanted to answer the question that they, themselves, had asked. When all was said and done, they solved the frosting problem (She used just short of 1,100 square inches of frosting!), and then we spent the rest of the class talking about our actual lesson for the day, which was on probability.

The geometry warm-up hadn't been connected to the day's topic, but class that day was lively and interesting, and my students were focused on identifying the important characteristics of the problem, gathering useful information, calculating it, and discussing what they'd found. They were living in the context of the problem that they'd asked me, not one I'd asked them. I could have presented the problem to them the way you and I would have received it in high school, but that would have been boring and completely irrelevant. Here is the old way of asking the birthday cake question:

Use the figure below to find the surface area of the birthday cake.

(Hint: the surface area of a cylinder = $2\pi r^2 + \pi r^2 h$.)

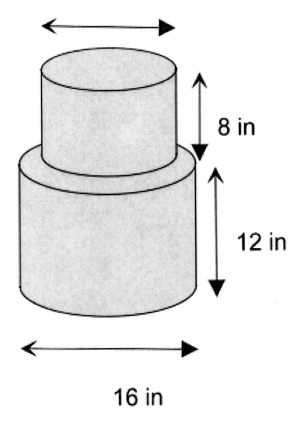

8 in

12 in

16 in

Lesson 2: The Language Arts One

Poetry was always one of my favorite units in English. I like how writing a poem gives you the freedom to express what you feel (and want to feel), what you think, and what you see, while being as vague as you choose to be. So when I showed the cake photo to one of my colleagues in the English department, she decided on the spot to use it as a poetry prompt. "This picture can evoke so much," she said. "I'd like to see where my students go with it." So she showed it to her class and gave two guidelines: First, look at the picture for one minute without taking your eyes off of it. Second, at the end of the minute, identify your feelings and write a poem in the shape of the birthday cake itself.

What an amazing assignment, to realize students could access their backgrounds, assumptions, and emotions through spending a little time with a picture. Afterward, she told me her students had written poems describing happiness, excess, sadness, wealth, poverty, Disney, science, history, love, hate, and powerlessness. With my colleague's permission, I want to share with you my favorite submission from the assignment:

I

am

an

Ame

rican

Girl!

A problem

that I know nothing of

brought me to this country.

Now I am an American Girl,

just like all of the other girls.

Isn't that what being an American Girl is?

If I am different, people ask me questions,

but don't want to get to know the real me.

But if I spend all my time trying to fit in then

who is the real me anyway? American Girl?

What does it mean to be an American Girl in an American Girl world?

Honestly, it means that humanness trumps background. Know people!

It means that "acceptance" and "tolerance" are swears. Substitute love.

It means loving myself, loving others who love me, and those who don't.

It means seeing people as someone important, not just as someone else.

I'm an American Girl now. The new version of an authentic American Girl.

—Anonymous

Thinking Questions

1. Do you have a personal photo that could inspire a good question or great writing? Are you willing to show it to your students?

2. What moments from your life, your weekend, your evenings are you already sharing with your students in everyday conversation? How could you share those moments in an educational context?

Listen Carefully

I like sports. The excitement of a competition fuels my own competitiveness, whether I'm running, playing tennis, tackling my two-year-old every time she comes within six feet of me, or aggressively going after the last barbecue chicken wing (I'm working on it.). As my body ages and my hamstrings become increasingly inflexible, though, I'm realizing I should stick to *watching* the more physical sports like football (not fútbol). That's why, instead of continuing to pursue my childhood dream of one day becoming a kicker for the NFL, I now watch football on my couch. (If a team loses their kicker and they call me up, I'll be ready!)

One Monday morning while listening to *SportsCenter* on ESPN Radio, I heard good-old, excitable sportscaster Chris Berman talking about a great catch that a wide receiver had made when he said, "He went up and caught the ball at its highest point!"

Berman had said this phrase multiple times on past shows, but a few of his other comments that day had already annoyed me, heightening my awareness of my disappointment with the statement. It made me think for a minute about math—of course—and, more specifically, a parabola and the football's projectile path.

Sometimes, my moments of connection aren't inspired by positive events, but rather come from being annoyed. I've found we often become more passionate about topics we're annoyed by because we intrinsically desire to voice our opinion on that topic. That was definitely the case for me here. I'd had enough of this *highest point* business.

The Berman was talking about a forty-two-yard pass. My basic understanding of football lends me to believe the throw illustrated here generally occurs when a pass is made.

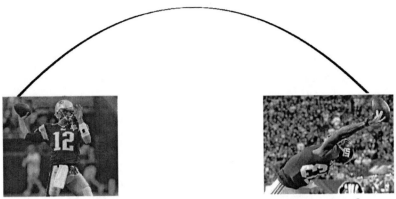

Tom Brady passes to Odell Beckham Jr ... Annoyed yet?

Now that we've gotten the complicated physics out of the way, after I shared my Berman frustrations with my students, I asked them, "What should Berman have said? Mathematically back up your statement." I'm sure you can imagine the discussion, argument, pencil pushing, and satisfaction that came from spending forty-five minutes to prove a famous person wrong. Ultimately, my students decided Berman should either revise his statement to "He caught it at its *lowest* point," or if the receiver had jumped to make the catch, "He caught it at *his* highest point." But what left me speechless was right before the bell rang, my students asked me, "Can we find other things sportspeople and news-people say that don't make sense and prove them wrong again? Maybe we can send them our work!" Let me be clear. They. Asked. Me. For. Homework.

Mission accomplished.

Thinking Questions

1. Is there something that bothers, irritates, or annoys you? Could you turn it from a negative into a positive in class?

2. Describe a homework assignment that your students might ask you for. Would you give it to them?

Snack Time

My wife is a wonderful woman who does wonderful things for our wonderful children (I hope she's reading this.). But no matter how hard she tries, when I come home from work, my kids run to hug me as if I'm returning from being away on a fishing boat for six months. She could be in the kitchen, holding homemade, freshly baked cookies on solid-gold plates, but if I came in with half a granola bar that I was willing to share, they would yell, "Fun Dad! Wooo!" She has come to terms with the arrangement (or so she tells me after a glass of wine).

One day I came home a little early, and my oldest daughter was at the kitchen table. As previously described, she ran up with a huge hug for Fun Dad but quickly expressed that she had a hunger that just wouldn't quit. I didn't have any Snickers bars available, but I did have a bag of M&M's, which I was glad to give her so I could retain my Fun Dad status. I was about to hand her the bag when, having a moment of awareness, I suddenly pulled the bag back and said, "Before I give this to you, tell me what's in the bag." Initially, she sarcastically answered, "M&M's," but after I stared her down, she elaborated: "It's candy. Chocolate, with a shell that's candy or might be candy. And they're colorful."

Since my daughter lives with me pretty much all the time (hooray for sleepovers), she knew this was headed toward math. So when I asked, "How many of each color do you think are in there?" she actually perked up. "I think there are thirty M&M's in there, and that makes five of each color!" she responded. The best part of the entire situation was that to validate her guess, all it took was giving her the bag to tear open and count. Turns out, there were fifty-four M&M's and significantly different totals for each color. That afternoon, she did Internet searches to find out information about M&M's colors and why companies like the Mars Corporation don't use an equal color distribution. She even texted her friends quickly to see what their favorite M&M color was. My realization that at that moment I should ask a question about the candy before just handing it over led to her discovering information, which, in turn, became a great middle-school statistics lesson. *Fun Dad! Wooo!*

────── Thinking Questions ──────

1. Has anything become so second nature that you miss the opportunity to add discovery to it?

2. Do you give your students a chance to guess and then search for their answers? Or is the answer more important in your classroom?

INSTANT

National Events and Crazes

*To me, the real state of the union is how
Americans react to current events.*

— *Henry Rollins*

Everyone knows about national events like the Super Bowl, presidential elections, and the State of the Union address. Likewise, we all know about the Ice Bucket Challenge, the Grammy Awards and Academy Awards, *Star Wars* releases, and "Weird Al" Yankovic's tour dates (well, maybe not that last one, but it's important to *me*). But when our students bring up these events or crazes in class, we often squash them by saying, "You can talk about that after class." Instead of sidelining the topics captivating my students' attention in favor of ones they struggle to stay awake through, I prefer to use them to instruct and connect.

When our students bring up these events or crazes in class, we often squash them by saying, "You can talk about that after class."

The Logo Game

Warning: this is a mathal (it's a word) section.

Remember the Logos Quiz hysteria of 2010? Of course you do. The Logo Quiz smartphone app removed all of a logo's identifying words and characteristics and then challenged players to guess which company the logo belonged to based on the shape of the remaining image. For me, the game was more than just an opportunity to show off how much television I'd watched as a kid—it was a chance to recognize the regular use of mathematical transformations to define images. In other words, it was a chance to notice that many logos are designs made of one shape that has been copied and moved around until the final logo is formed.

Since my students at the time were avidly playing the game, I made an activity using company logos for my Algebra 2 students: I gave the class a logo on a coordinate plane and defined a portion of it as the shape called f(x). From there, they needed to identify how the other portion of the logo got there by using transformations (mathematical shifts).

For example, I outlined the left side of the Mazda logo in red (left) and then asked students how to make the blue side (right) from the red. Simple answer, y= f(x) is red so y= f(-x) is blue.

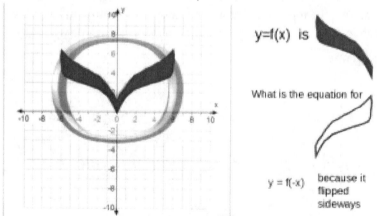

Transformations...More Than Meets the Eye

I did this with several more logos, including Buick and Hyundai.

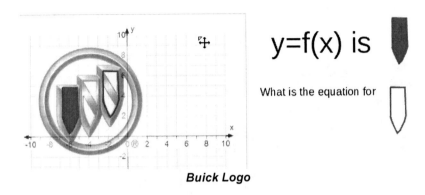

Buick Logo

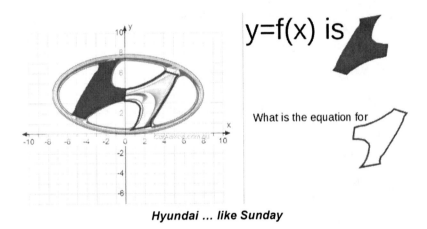

Hyundai ... like Sunday

My students had fun working on these graphs, and it helped them see transformations in their everyday lives, which led to the best part of the activity: the blank page at the end. As I mentioned earlier, my students were heavily into the Logo Quiz game, so as an exit ticket from class, I had them play the game in pairs on their phones (to alleviate phone shortages) in class, but not so they could win and compare scores. Instead, I wanted them to identify the transformations on the logos. The students e-mailed me screenshots of their favorite logos, and the next day's warm-up included their transformations. I loved this activity, and so did my students. I had given them a few logo examples in class that day, but the game gave them so many more to analyze.

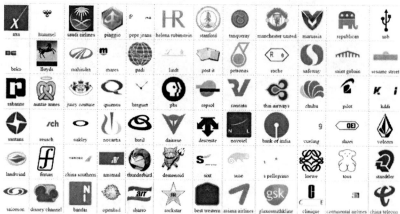

Spoiler Alert! Answers to Logo Quiz App

—————— Thinking Questions ——————

1. Which non-educational smartphone app or game could you use as a teaching tool?

2. In what ways can you create cross-curricular connections from lessons like this?

The State of the Union Address

At least once a year, the president of the United States (POTUS) delivers a State of the Union (SOTU) address to the American people (SKEPTICAL). I refuse to get political here, as my votes typically go to the candidates who support my interest in increasing the number of public trampolines nationwide. But when I asked the teachers at my lunch table how they'd use the POTUS' SOTU address in their classes, they suggested the following (in no particular order):

- Choose a numerical claim the president made and fact-check it.
- Analyze the types of words used, keeping track of the number of letters. For example, does President Obama use larger words than former President George W. Bush?
- Identify the SOTU address's figures of speech, including metaphors, hyperbole, euphemism, etc.
- Choose a paragraph from the SOTU address and have students rearrange its subjects and predicates to make a new paragraph that makes sense but conveys a totally different message. (I love this one. I called it the "That's Not What I Said!" assignment.)
- Write a sonnet or other type of poem using sentences from the SOTU address with the appropriate meter and rhyme.
- Discuss the environmental impact that would result if at least one of the president's promises came to fruition.
- Compare the promises this president gave in his SOTU address with SOTU addresses given twenty-five, fifty, and seventy-five years ago. How were they similar? Do we have the same problems?
- Make a SOTU address highlight reel, ESPN-style.
- Create a soundtrack for the speech using GarageBand or another digital music creator.

Thinking Questions

1. Can you come up with a few more ideas your students can use to make the speech relevant to their learning?

2. How could you use a major and sometimes controversial event to your students' benefit?

INSTANT
Two or More Content Areas

My greatest benefit gained from school was an initiation into the love of learning, of learning how to learn ... as a matter of interdisciplinary cognition—that is, learning to know something by its relation to something else.

—Leonard Bernstein

As you've been reading, you've probably noticed that connecting with our students in a relevant way often means going beyond our content area to effectively engage students in learning our content area. For example, earlier in this book, I shared with you how one teacher used art and physics in the Calder mobile, as well as other stories that incorporate poetry, music, social studies, technology, environmental science, and culinary arts. Too often, we forget that each day our students have many different classes and engage in learning about many different subjects. To focus only on our own content is to miss an opportunity to create a connection, one that could lead to a moment that locks in a concept or an idea for our students. This section discusses opportunities to create and plan lessons—not just react to situations—that open the doors to long-lasting meaning for students.

Crowdsourced Creativity

Like many of you, I enjoy reading and participating in Twitter chats. In fact, you may have even heard about this book through a Twitter chat. The high-speed commentary flowing from passionate teachers and administrators fuels my own passion and gets my creative juices going.

I recently participated in a Twitter chat about Youth Art Month, and the discussion revolved around how we're promoting art, the arts, and students' growing desires to have art in education. During this short, one-hour chat, I was reminded of something I loved but hadn't done in a while; I remembered a time when a student inspired me greatly, and I came up with a new idea that happened to strike a chord with many of the educators also participating in the chat. Here are those three moments:

"I was reminded of something I loved but hadn't done in a while." First, if you haven't seen "blackout poetry," go look it up now. It's okay, I'll wait. *Tick-tock, tick-tock.* Welcome back! Isn't blackout poetry great? If you don't have access to Google at the moment, simply put, black-out poetry is when someone takes newspapers (those still exist), book pages, and other physical samples with words and blacks out words and sections, leaving behind only the text that makes up the poem.

Creating blackout poetry is an interesting way for students to discover value in text they may have initially dismissed entirely. I have students do this with pages from math textbooks (Yes, they still exist, too.), and you'd be surprised at the beauty, depth, and social commentary that can come from a page about graphing quadratic functions. Try creating a blackout poem for yourself, and then have your students try it. But don't give them rules. Some students may find poetry in blacking out every word, recognizing that silence speaks volumes, while others may not focus on the words at all, but instead focus on

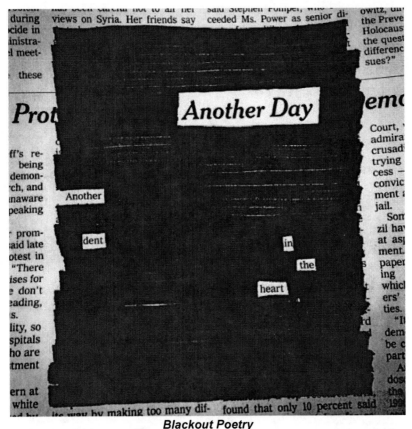

Blackout Poetry
One of Austin Kleon's newspaper blackout poems from his blog at
austinkleon.com, September 2, 2013 (reprinted with permission)

the blackout itself and create a wonderful drawing. Whatever your students create, put it up on the wall to display.

"I remembered a time when a student inspired me greatly." The high-school science department was doing a unit on water conservation for Earth Week. Students were to research major issues surrounding water in our country and in the world, analyze their information, and propose ideas for solving the problems they found. The art teacher, who knew the science department was doing this, gave her senior art students this assignment: create a piece titled "The Importance of Water." The rest was up to them.

Many of her students went down the route of showing desolate wastelands, dead fish, dry farms, and a heated earth, but a student from my math class painted the picture you see here.

Painting Titled, "The Importance of Water"

When I saw it, I'd never felt so pulled into an image. *That was me.* This captured moment was why water is important—to me. I bought this painting from my student, and I look at it every day, sometimes for too long.

"I came up with an idea that happened to strike a chord with many of the educators also participating in the chat." When the chat moderator asked, "How do you integrate technology with the arts?" many participants initially answered saying they post pictures and videos to their websites and to share with families. The stories then moved on to creating QR codes that link to their students' work. That's when it hit me: let's use QR code technology, but take it full circle. First, have students create art—whether it's two-dimensional, three-dimensional, a musical performance, a graphic design, dance, a video, or anything else—and then digitize it and link it to a QR code. Afterward, create an image using all of the students' QR codes and display it in the school. Parents can then scan each QR code when they visit. This is an example of a possibility.

Code Made of QR codes

Students create the art and connect it to the technology, which, in turn, becomes the art itself.

> ## Life's Masterpiece
>
> Consider the Mona Lisa. DaVinci deeply understood each color he used to paint her. School subjects are each colors: Math, red...Science, green, etc...each lesson deepening our understanding of the nuance of each color, not so that we may recreate the Mona Lisa, but so that we may paint *Our Own Picture*.
>
> —*Denis Sheeran*
> *Teacher, Father, Mathematician, Life Painter*

Thinking Questions

1. Have you incorporated art into other disciplines? If so, how?

2. When a student inspires you, how do you react?

3. How could you take your ideas for interdisciplinary connections a step further?

Poetry in Motion

I was talking to an English teacher friend one day, when our conversation turned to integrating technology into a poetry assignment. In her mind, poetry and technology simply didn't mix. She'd always given her students a prompt, such as a painting, a sentence, or an emotion, and then sent them off to write a specific type of poem. So when she asked me how to integrate technology into her students' writing, I suggested she ask them to capture a moment with their phone's camera and then write a poem about it. Simple. As we were walking to our cars from the school building, she saw fresh snow, glistening on a tree branch. At that moment, she stopped and took a picture of the branch, which she then used as her poetry prompt.

She didn't know it, but while she was taking her picture of the snow, I was taking a picture of her taking a picture of the snow (go back and read it again—got it?). For her, the poetry of the moment was in the nature, but for me, the poetry was how she noticed the opportunity she wanted her students to notice.

There will always be multiple perspectives on every moment, so when you find a relevant moment to bring into your classroom, don't forget to share it with your colleagues or school's student leaders. Their views will not only help you clarify an idea but can also enhance its relevance to your students.

When my English teacher friend presented the poetry lesson to her students, she read the poem she'd written, which turned out beautifully. Her ability to use words to spark the imagination far exceeds that of most people I've met. When she finished, I asked if I could read a poem I'd written. She was happy to oblige because she knew the additional example could help her class.

I see you. I am here.

Do you see what I see?

I see what you see, and I see you.

You see beauty, enough to capture it.

I see the chase, the catch, the reward.

You exist in your moment. I exist in mine, because of you.

We move to leave the cold. The cold, which brought us the moment.

What will you do with it? What will they? What have I done?

What have I done?

I see you.

I am here.

Who sees me?

Instantly, she knew the moment I'd written about. When I showed her students the picture I'd taken, they understood how our poems were describing our different perspectives on a single moment. My colleague later told me that the poems her students had written for that lesson were among the richest she'd received in many years. I attribute this entirely to her willingness to grow and share moments with her class. It was great to be a part of that experience.

Humorist Jack Handey wrote, "Before you criticize a man, walk a mile in his shoes. That way, when you do criticize him, you'll be a mile away and have his shoes."[1] Not much of that quote really applies to this situation, other than "walk a mile in his shoes," but I like it nonetheless. Take time to view your teaching from your students' perspectives, through the lens of their learning.

Take time to view your teaching from your students' perspectives, through the lens of their learning.

Thinking Questions

1. Are you teaching something relevant to you and your interests?

2. Do you tap other professionals inside and outside of your school and ask for their perspectives? What could you learn by doing this?

---

1   Jack Handey, "Jack Handey Quote," izquotes.com, 2016, http://izquotes.com/quote/296418

Getting There

Thomas Edison said, "I have not failed. I've just found 10,000 ways that won't work."[1] And that's stuck with me. It's the perfect quote to lead you into a discussion about design, professional development, or lesson planning. But I'm not going there. In fact, sometimes I don't know where I'm going at all, which is exactly where I'm going (stick with me, we'll get there).

Before GPS and Google Maps, I got lost—a lot. If Thomas Edison were alive, he might say, "He hasn't gotten lost. He's just found 10,000 ways that don't lead to where he wanted to go" (actual quote, verification pending). But without my poor decision-making and lack of an intrinsic "true north," I more than likely never would have stopped at the best diner in Britt, Iowa, or Clyde Peeling's Reptiland in Allenwood, Pennsylvania, or The Wonder Spot in the Wisconsin Dells, Wisconsin. But I *did* stop at all of these places, and I learned something interesting while visiting each of them. For example, Britt hosts a hobo convention each year, boa constrictors don't like to be poked with sticks, and The Wonder Spot is difficult to describe. Chances are, if you've read this far, then you may actually be considering trying some of the ideas and techniques I've discussed during our time together but may be wondering where to start. Allow Google Maps to help.

---

1   Thomas Edison, "Thomas A. Edison Quotes," brainyquote.com, 2016, http://www.brainyquote.com/quotes/quotes/t/thomasaed132683.html

Next is a map of potential directions from Britt, Iowa, to The Wonder Spot in the Wisconsin Dells. (In case you were wondering, this trip is totally worth the drive.)

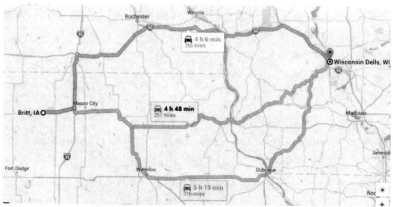

Directions from Here to There

The really interesting thing here is that Google doesn't know you or your travel preferences (for now), so it gives you choices. There's the direct route, which takes you straight ahead; the highlighted one, which is the fastest but unexpectedly takes you through Minnesota; and then there's the third route, which adds more than fifty miles to your trip and highlights such traditional Iowa attractions as Dubuque and corn. When you're considering how to use your days, nights, and class time, there's one thing I can tell you for sure: as this map illustrates, there's no one way to do it. You may be the direct route type, preferring to find the easiest way to integrate your moments into the learning process; you may opt for the fastest route so you can jump right in and try anything; or you may opt for the scenic route, wanting to see a lesson in action first, step back to take it all in, and maybe try a little here and there until you're ready to dive in.

Whichever type of person you are, this one thing is true: We have no choice but to make learning more relevant to our students, or they will learn without us. Some of education's best minds are sharing their resources on the Internet, including virtual courseware, online tutors, and textbooks, making individualized, self-paced learning easier than ever. So what can we as teachers offer our students that "massive open online courses" (MOOCS) and online tutorials can't? Relevance. Together, let's change "When am I going to use this in real life?" to "Which part of your life did you get this from?" And this time, let's have an answer.

Acknowledgments

I would like to thank the following people, whose support in writing this book has made it no longer necessary for me to tell strangers about the time I graphed my food.

To my wife, Carrie, thank you for encouraging me to keep writing, laughing at my jokes (some of which made it into the book), and for giving me time and snacks to keep me going during the process.

To my children, Ellie, Katie, Danny and Lily, thank you for going to bed early enough for me to get some work done every now and then and for playing the role of Best Supporting Actors in this book.

To Dave and Shelley Burgess, thank you for, in one conversation, taking an idea for a book about math lessons and drawing out what I was really trying to say and then giving me the chance to say it.

To Alice Keeler, thank you for saying, "I love your ideas; you have to talk to Shelley Burgess!"

And a special thanks to all the students and teachers who connected with my stories, shared their own, inspired me to look at the world differently, and learned with me along the way.

Bring the *Instant Relevance* Message to Your District, Organization, or Event!

Denis Sheeran is available to speak at conferences, workshops, and events. As a keynote speaker, Denis can tailor professional development training to the needs of your district and is happy to learn alongside you.

Denis regularly presents professional development on the following themes:

- Instant Relevance: How to incorporate the Instant Relevance message in the classroom and the entire district
- From Do Now to Think Now: Engaging students from the moment class starts
- Google Apps in the Math Classroom for beginners
- Google Apps in the Math Classroom: Taking it to the Next Level
- Google Apps in the General Classroom: For Beginners and The Next Level
- Using Unanswerable Questions to Build Statistical Thinkers
- Harnessing the Power of Chromebooks

More From

Teach Like a PIRATE

*Increase Student Engagement, Boost Your
Creativity, and Transform Your Life as an Educator*

By Dave Burgess (@BurgessDave)

Teach Like a PIRATE is the *New York Times'* best-selling book that has sparked a worldwide educational revolution. It is part inspirational manifesto that ignites passion for the profession, and part practical road map filled with dynamic strategies to dramatically increase student engagement. Translated into multiple languages, its message resonates with educators who want to design outrageously creative lessons and transform school into a life-changing experience for students.

Learn Like a PIRATE

*Empower Your Students to Collaborate,
Lead, and Succeed*

By Paul Solarz (@PaulSolarz)

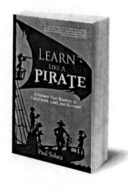

Today's job market demands that students be prepared to take responsibility for their lives and careers. We do them a disservice if we teach them how to earn passing grades without equipping them to take charge of their education. In *Learn Like a PIRATE*, Paul Solarz explains how to design classroom experiences that encourage students to take risks and explore their passions in a stimulating, motivating, and supportive environment where improvement, rather than grades, is the focus. Discover how student-led classrooms help students thrive and develop into self-directed, confident citizens who are capable of making smart, responsible decisions, all on their own.

P is for PIRATE

Inspirational ABC's for Educators

By Dave and Shelley Burgess (@Burgess_Shelley)

Teaching is an adventure that stretches the imagination and calls for creativity every day! In *P is for Pirate*, husband and wife team, Dave and Shelley Burgess, encourage and inspire educators to make their classrooms fun and exciting places to learn. Tapping into years of personal experience and drawing on the insights of more than seventy educators, the authors offer a wealth of ideas for making learning and teaching more fulfilling than ever before.

Play Like a Pirate

Engage Students with Toys, Games, and Comics

by Quinn Rollins (@jedikermit)

Yes! School can be simultaneously fun and educational. In *Play Like a Pirate*, Quinn Rollins offers practical, engaging strategies and resources that make it easy to integrate fun into your curriculum. Regardless of the grade level you teach, you'll find inspiration and ideas that will help you engage your students in unforgettable ways.

eXPlore Like a Pirate

Gamification and Game-Inspired Course Design to Engage, Enrich, and Elevate Your Learners

By Michael Matera (@MrMatera)

Are you ready to transform your classroom into an experiential world that flourishes on collaboration and creativity? Then set sail with classroom game designer and educator Michael Matera as he reveals the possibilities and power of game-based learning. In *eXPlore Like a Pirate*, Matera serves as your experienced guide to help you apply the most motivational techniques of gameplay to your classroom. You'll learn gamification strategies that will work with and enhance (rather than replace) your current curriculum and discover how these engaging methods can be applied to any grade level or subject.

Pure Genius

Building a Culture of Innovation and
Taking 20% Time to the Next Level

By Don Wettrick (@DonWettrick)

For far too long, schools have been bastions of boredom, killers of creativity, and way too comfortable with compliance and conformity. In *Pure Genius*, Don Wettrick explains how collaboration—with experts, students, and other educators—can help you create interesting, and even life-changing, opportunities for learning. Wettrick's book inspires and equips educators with a systematic blueprint for teaching innovation in any school.

The Zen Teacher

Creating Focus, Simplicity, and
Tranquility in the Classroom

By Dan Tricarico (@thezenteacher)

Teachers have incredible power to influence—even improve—the future. In *The Zen Teacher*, educator, blogger, and speaker Dan Tricarico provides practical, easy-to-use techniques to help teachers be their best—unrushed and fully focused—so they can maximize their performance and improve their quality of life. In this introductory guide, Dan Tricarico explains what it means to develop a Zen practice—something that has nothing to do with religion and everything to do with your ability to thrive in the classroom.

140 Twitter Tips for Educators

Get Connected, Grow Your Professional Learning
Network, and Reinvigorate Your Career

By Brad Currie, Billy Krakower, and Scott Rocco
(@bradmcurrie, @wkrakower, @ScottRRocco)

Whatever questions you have about education or about how you can be even better at your job, you'll find ideas, resources, and a vibrant network of professionals ready to help you on Twitter. In *140 Twitter Tips for Educators*, #Satchat hosts and founders of Evolving Educators, Brad Currie, Billy Krakower, and Scott Rocco offer step-by-step instructions to help you master the basics of Twitter, build an online following, and become a Twitter rock star.

The Innovator's Mindset

Empower Learning, Unleash Talent,
and Lead a Culture of Creativity

By George Couros (@gcouros)

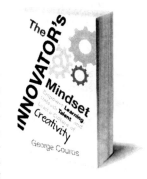

The traditional system of education requires students to hold their questions and compliantly stick to the scheduled curriculum. But our job as educators is to provide new and better opportunities for our students. It's time to recognize that compliance doesn't foster innovation, encourage critical thinking, or inspire creativity—and those are the skills our students need to succeed. In *The Innovator's Mindset*, George Couros encourages teachers and administrators to empower their learners to wonder, to explore—and to become forward-thinking leaders.

50 Things You Can Do with Google Classroom

By Alice Keeler and Libbi Miller
(@alicekeeler, @MillerLibbi)

It can be challenging to add new technology to the classroom but it's a must if students are going to be well-equipped for the future. Alice Keeler and Libbi Miller shorten the learning curve by providing a thorough overview of the Google Classroom App. Part of Google Apps for Education (GAfE), Google Classroom was specifically designed to help teachers save time by streamlining the process of going digital. Complete with screenshots, *50 Things You Can Do with Google Classroom* provides ideas and step-by-step instructions to help teachers implement this powerful tool.

50 Things to Go Further with Google Classroom

A Student-Centered Approach
By Alice Keeler and Libbi Miller
(@alicekeeler, @MillerLibbi)

Today's technology empowers educators to move away from the traditional classroom where teachers lead and students work independently—each doing the same thing. In 50 Things to Go Further with Google Classroom: A Student-Centered Approach, authors and educators Alice Keeler and Libbi Miller offer inspiration and resources to help you create a digitally rich, engaging, student-centered environment. They show you how to tap into the power of individualized learning that is possible with Google Classroom.

Master the Media

*How Teaching Media Literacy Can
Save Our Plugged-in World*

By Julie Smith (@julnilsmith)

Written to help teachers and parents educate the next generation, *Master the Media* explains the history, purpose, and messages behind the media. The point isn't to get kids to unplug; it's to help them make informed choices, understand the difference between truth and lies, and discern perception from reality. Critical thinking leads to smarter decisions—and it's why media literacy can save the world.

The Writing on the Classroom Wall

*How Posting Your Most Passionate Beliefs about
Education Can Empower Your Students, Propel Your
Growth, and Lead to a Lifetime of Learning*

By Steve Wyborney (@SteveWyborney)

In *The Writing on the Classroom Wall*, Steve Wyborney explains how posting and discussing Big Ideas can lead to deeper learning. You'll learn why sharing your ideas will sharpen and refine them. You'll also be encouraged to know that the Big Ideas you share don't have to be profound to make a profound impact on learning. In fact, Steve explains, it's okay if some of your ideas fall *off* the wall. What matters most is sharing them.

Kids Deserve It!

*Pushing Boundaries and Challenging
Conventional Thinking*

By Todd Nesloney and Adam Welcome
(@TechNinjaTodd, @awelcome)

In *Kids Deserve It!*, Todd and Adam encourage you to think big and make learning fun and meaningful for students. Their high-tech, high-touch, and highly engaging practices will inspire you to take risks, shake up the status quo, and be a champion for your students. While you're at it, you just might rediscover why you became an educator in the first place.

The Classroom Chef

Sharpen your lessons. Season your classes.
Make math meaningful.

By John Stevens and Matt Vaudrey
(@Jstevens009, @MrVaudrey)

In *The Classroom Chef*, math teachers and instructional coaches John Stevens and Matt Vaudrey share their secret recipes, ingredients, and tips for serving up lessons that engage students and help them "get" math. You can use these ideas and methods as-is, or better yet, tweak them and create your own enticing educational meals. The message the authors share is that, with imagination and preparation, every teacher can be a Classroom Chef.

Ditch That Textbook

Free Your Teaching and Revolutionize
Your Classroom

By Matt Miller (@jmattmiller)

Textbooks are symbols of centuries-old education. They're often outdated as soon as they hit students' desks. Acting "by the textbook" implies compliance and a lack of creativity. It's time to ditch those textbooks—and those textbook assumptions about learning! In *Ditch That Textbook*, teacher and blogger Matt Miller encourages educators to throw out meaningless, pedestrian teaching and learning practices. He empowers them to evolve and improve on old, standard, teaching methods. *Ditch That Textbook* is a support system, toolbox, and manifesto to help educators free their teaching and revolutionize their classrooms.

How Much Water Do We Have?

*5 Success Principles for Conquering Any
Change and Thriving in Times of Change*

By Pete Nunweiler with Kris Nunweiler

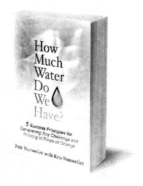

In *How Much Water Do We Have?* Pete Nunweiler identifies five key elements—information, planning, motivation, support, and leadership—that are necessary for the success of any goal, life transition, or challenge. Referring to these elements as the 5 Waters of Success, Pete explains that like the water we drink, you need them to thrive in today's rapidly paced world. If you're feeling stressed out, overwhelmed, or uncertain at work or at home, pause and look for the signs of dehydration. Learn how to find, acquire, and use the 5 Waters of Success—so you can share them with your team and family members.

Launch

*Using Design Thinking to Boost Creativity
and Bring Out the Maker in Every Student*

By John Spencer and A.J. Juliani (@spencerideas, @ajjuliani)

Something happens in students when they define themselves as *makers* and *inventors* and *creators*. They discover powerful skills—problem-solving, critical thinking, and imagination—that will help them shape the world's future ... *our* future. In *LAUNCH*, John Spencer and A.J. Juliani provide a process that can be incorporated into every class at every grade level ... even if you don't consider yourself a "creative teacher." And if you dare to innovate and view creativity as an essential skill, you will empower your students to change the world—starting right now.

Your School Rocks ... So Tell People!

Passionately Pitch and Promote the Positives Happening on Your Campus

By Ryan McLane and Eric Lowe
(@McLane_Ryan, @EricLowe21)

Great things are happening in your school every day. The problem is, no one beyond your school walls knows about them. School principals Ryan McLane and Eric Lowe want to help you get the word out! In *Your School Rocks ... So Tell People!* McLane and Lowe offer more than seventy immediately actionable tips along with easy-to-follow instructions and links to video tutorials. This practical guide will equip you to create an effective and manageable communication strategy using social media tools. Learn how to keep your students' families and community connected, informed, and excited about what's going on in your school.

About the Author

Denis Sheeran is an engaging, fun, highly requested nationwide speaker, who delivers keynotes, full-day workshops, and small-group professional development courses to teachers and administrators. He is a Google Certified Educator, Chromebook in the Classroom trainer, Smartboard and Smart Notebook trainer, and can customize PD for your school district. Denis developed a course for his future non-math majors called Senior Math Topics, which covered a range of topics from the mathematics of music and art to modern encryption, machine design, and the history of mathematics. He also enjoys helping educators develop new courses and curricula to fit the needs of diverse student populations.

Denis has a master's degree in educational leadership and a bachelor's degree in mathematics education with a minor in music. He is an adjunct professor of statistics at the County College of Morris in Randolph, New Jersey. Before becoming the supervisor of mathematics for K–12 students in Chatham, New Jersey, Denis taught high school math, from Algebra to Advanced Placement, for thirteen years at Lake Forest High School in Lake Forest, Illinois.

Denis is a certified online and hybrid course teacher and has been asked to serve on the statistics development committee by several online course companies. He was most recently published in the fall 2015 Statistics Teacher Network Journal. Denis lives in New Jersey with his wife, four children, and his litter-box-trained dog, Scout.

 @MathDenisNJ

denissheeran.com

CPSIA information can be obtained
at www.ICGtesting.com
Printed in the USA
FFOW02n2203231017
41451FF

9 780996 989596